"Karl Schultz provides a valuable resource for men, women, and teenagers to become aware of the distress inherent in our fast-paced lives. He convinces us of the wisdom of redirecting our thoughts, emotions, and actions; in essence, we are rediscovering our spiritual Christ-like natures. We learn practical ways to slow down; to open our eyes, hearts, minds, and spirits; and to become more peaceful and balanced. If individuals begin to live the truths presented here, then our present and future world holds bright promise for us all." **Diane M. Fletcher, MA, RN, OCN,** nurse clinician, University of Pittsburgh Cancer Institute

"Here is a book for the person who thinks that stress management is devoid of spiritual significance. Schultz speaks about the human and the Divine in a way that makes you feel at home. Using the wisdom of the ages, he helps us keep our eyes on Jesus as the storm swirls around us." **Fr. Scott Seethaler, OFM Cap.,** Catholic evangelist

"This book is a must-read for all who face the daily reality of stress. Concise, well written, and well documented, it should be added to any Christian family's library. If taken a chapter or two per night, it can be read in as little as a week, but the thought process and knowledge it contains could easily last a lifetime and serve as a failproof system for stress management." **Jim Harris,** president, Princeton Product and Consulting, Chelsea, OK

"Karl Schultz seeks to help others find uncomplicated paths for peace of heart. His disarmingly simple methods can lead a Christian to follow a way of reflection, inspiration, and inner quiet by faithful spiritual reading. Without ponderous explanations, he presents knowledge that will help Christians contemplate, in and through our real lives, inspired by the word." **Fr. Robert L. McCreary, OFM Cap.,** Saint Mary's Seminary, Wickliffe, OH

"Stress comes from living as if we control our own little world. We often forget that there is an essence far more knowledgeable than we are. *Calming the Stormy Seas of Stress* not only reminds us of the fruits provided to us by living through the Holy Spirit—love, joy, peace, patience, kindness, goodness, faithfulness, gentleness, and self-control—it also shows us the path to reflect, absorb, and give our lives back into the Holy Spirit's hands. Most important, it reminds us that loving our neighbors brings so much more to our lives than striving to be better than them, and that even in today's world inner peace, fellowship, and happiness are ours if we ask." **Amy Skolen, MBA,** management consultant, Strategic Solutions

Calming
the
Stormy Seas
of Stress

Karl A. Schultz

Director, Genesis Personal Development Center
3431 Gass Avenue
Pittsburgh, PA 15212
412-766-7545

Foreword by Timothy Fitzgerald, CP

Saint Mary's Press
Christian Brothers Publications
Winona, Minnesota

Genuine recycled paper with 10% post-consumer waste.
Printed with soy-based ink.

The publishing team included Michael Wilt, development editor; Rebecca
Fairbank, manuscript editor; Hollace Storkel, typesetter; Maurine R. Twait, art
director; Cindi Ramm, cover designer; cover photograph by Ernst Haas, Tony
Stone Images; pre-press, printing, and binding by the graphics division of Saint
Mary's Press.

The Scripture quotations herein are from the New Revised Standard Version
of the Bible. Copyright © 1989 by the Division of Christian Education of the
National Council of the Churches of Christ in the United States of America.
Used by permission. All rights reserved.
    The extract on page 8 by Pope Paul VI is from *L'Osservatore Romano*, 24
April 1969.
    The excerpt by Pope Paul VI on page 9 is from *The Teachings of Pope Paul
VI* (Washington, DC: United States Catholic Conference [USCC], 1971), page
273. Copyright © 1971 by the USCC.
    The Serenity Prayer, by Reinhold Niebuhr, on pages 57–58 is quoted from
*Familiar Quotations: A Collection of Passages, Phrases, and Proverbs Traced to
Their Sources in Ancient and Modern Literature*, fifteenth and one-hundred and
twenty-fifth anniversary edition, by John Bartlett (Boston: Little, Brown and
Company, 1980), page 823. Copyright © 1980 by Little, Brown and Company.
    The excerpt on page 65 is from *The Cloud of Unknowing*, edited with an
introduction by James Walsh, SJ (New York: Paulist Press, 1981), page 148.
Copyright © 1981 by the Missionary Society of Saint Paul the Apostle in the
State of New York.
    The excerpt by Francis de Sales on page 69 is from *Thy Will Be Done:
Letters to Persons in the World* (Manchester, NH: Sophia Institute Press, 1995),
page 49. Copyright © 1995 by Sophia Institute Press.

Printed in the United States of America

Printing: 9 8 7 6 5 4 3 2 1

Year: 2007 06 05 04 03 02 01 00 99

ISBN 0-88489-584-X

Contents

Foreword by Timothy Fitzgerald, CP   7

Introduction   9

Reflections on Being and Doing   15

1. Affirmation   16
2. Prayer   18
3. Silence   20
4. Counsel   22
5. Anger   24
6. Coping with Criticism   26
7. Proportion   28
8. Perspective   30
9. Awareness   32
10. Discernment   34
11. Dialogue   36
12. Common Sense   38
13. Tolerance   40
14. Ordered Sensuality   41
15. Simplicity   43
16. Shabbat   45
17. Gratitude   47
18. Generosity and Detachment   49
19. Peacemaking   51
20. Fiscal Prudence   53
21. Humor   55
22. Acceptance   57
23. Choosing Our Company   59
24. Compassion and Service   61

25. Creativity   *63*
26. Humility   *65*
27. Living in the Present   *67*
28. Patience and Perseverance   *69*

Reflections on Lifestyle Issues and Activities   *71*

29. Music   *72*
30. Boredom Busters   *74*
31. Rut Breakers   *76*

Reflections on Moderation and Balance   *79*

32. Sleep   *80*
33. Work and Play   *82*
34. Diet   *85*
35. Exercise   *87*
36. Family Values   *89*
37. Permission and Prohibition   *91*

Closing Synthesis   *94*

Bibliography   *95*

Foreword

Karl Schultz has addressed in this book one of the primary challenges of living in a technological and permissive society: how to live peacefully with God and neighbor in our world today. Our so-called labor-saving devices have not created true leisure but rather an intrusion into our sacred space. Our information superhighway, or data smog as some call it, has not advanced genuine study, prayer, good conversation, or wisdom. Our silence spaces are filled with noise, extroversion, and destructive recreations. Commonsense logic has broken down in marriage, dialogue, political life, and religion. An element of discontinuity has blinded many to the normal reasoning process and emotionally balanced responses. As a society, we are on a journey of road rage.

Genuine Christian spirituality is a journey not of rage and violence but of reverence and peace. We need meaningful work, meaningful liturgy, meaningful cultural and social surroundings. We journey both inward and outward: to the core of our being and to the cosmic reach of the universe under the headship of Christ. It is this experience of Christ, the center of our heart and the center of the universe, that suffuses all aspects of existence: self, world, people, friends, God. Peace resides in those who are true to their human and Christian vocation: to be contemplative, reverent worshipers.

In *Calming the Stormy Seas of Stress,* Schultz looks to the basic pattern of all contemplative experience, using skillfully, in modern language and experience, the insights of Guigo II in his *Ladder to Paradise:* reading divine signs, meditation, prayer, and contemplation. Schultz's great contribution here is to put the stress on reading divine signs (*lectio divina*) as an effective antidote to today's rush and rage. From the very rich menu of reflections on the sacred Scriptures and human experience that Schultz offers, I would like to concentrate on three areas: what *lectio* is, what *lectio* leads to, and the fruits of *lectio*.

Lectio divina is the art of reading and of listening, not only to words but also to all the other signs: nature, events, persons. Based on a sacramental view of the universe, we are invited to go beyond signs and symbols to God himself. This intuiting of the sacrament of the moment goes counter to today's sociocultural environment, which is so largely influenced by the work ethic, the need for success, the need to keep producing goods, the need to consume the universe until we have polluted all our natural transparencies of God. This is an age that wants to rush to relationships and hurry friendships. Reading divine things means to wait, to approach God, others, oneself, and one's work in reverence and not in rage. Tremendous rewards can be found in the patient demands of silent and wonder-filled listening.

This kind of reading leads naturally to a search for meaning in what one has "read." It truly is the reflective *now* drunk in. In more traditional language, we call this kind of reflection habitual recollection. Its whole purpose is to make us aware that God is truly present in all things. It is a faith reflection aided by all the experiences of our life with God. It is prayerfulness in all situations.

Pope Paul VI, in a memorable address on April 16, 1969, said:

> We can pass from the position of mere observers to that of critics, thinkers, judges. This attitude of reflective knowledge is of the greatest importance for the modern soul, if it wishes to remain a living soul, and not just a screen for the thousand impressions to which it is subject. . . . The discovery of the signs of the times is a fact of Christian conscience. It results from a comparison of faith with life; not to superimpose, artificially and superficially, a devout thought on the cases of our experience, but rather to see where these cases postulate, by their intrinsic dynamism, by their very obscurity, and sometimes by their very immorality, a ray of faith, an evangelical word, that classifies them, that redeems them.

The fruits of *lectio* come truly but not easily. This is not a how-to book with quick and ready solutions. Rather it is a workbook that draws out our own inner wisdom, demanding attention, reflection, and hard work. The results, under God's grace, are truly tremendous. We can see this in the "action responses" Schultz suggests, which could easily sound like daily astrological throwaways, but really after much work, yield richer and deeper penetration into one's own life.

You are in for a special treat in this book. Humility, acceptance, compassion, patience, and perseverance among so many others are all virtues requiring great inner calm and a supreme effort to eliminate the negative stressors in our life.

Timothy Fitzgerald, CP
Saint Paul's Monastery
Pittsburgh, Pennsylvania
Easter 1998

Introduction

Praying the Passion

Christian life is a paschal journey; we pass through suffering and stress en route to the cross and resurrection. God is the stress transformer par excellence. Pope Paul VI developed the insight that because Christ was so fully human, his experience and awareness of pain was keener than ours can be. Christ is thus eminently qualified to be our ultimate inspiration and authority on stress:

> Who has suffered as much as Jesus? Suffering is proportionate to two measures: sensibility (and what finer sensibility than that of Christ, the Man God?), and love: the capacity for love is measured by the capacity for suffering. (Paul VI, "Mass for Invalids from Roman Hospitals on the Feast of Corpus Domini," 10 June 1971)

Both the daily and major rejections and ambiguities that cause us so much stress were experienced intimately by Jesus during his Passion. Saints Augustine and Albert the Great, to name just two proponents, advocated reflection on the Passion as the highest of spiritual exercises. Reflection on the Passion can help us transform our stress as well. Viewed in light of the cross, our pains take on transcendent meaning.

The challenge for Christians is to identify the paschs in our lives that invite us to pass from the slavery of selfishness to the freedom of trusting obedience. By taking these paths and facing our problems, rather than hiding in power or control games or apathy, we let God redeem and transform our suffering.

We do not satisfy ourselves with merely coping with suffering and stress; we expect God to bring good out of it. This inspires and energizes us. But first we must differentiate suffering from stress.

Stress and Suffering

I often ask attendees at my stress transformation and suffering workshops to define and distinguish stress and suffering. The general understanding is that stress is a physiological and psychological reaction to some stimulus, whereas suffering is the spiritual and moral dimension of that reaction and its effects.

Pioneer researcher Hans Selye defines stress as a nonspecific response of the body to an external stimulus. He differentiates between good stress that arises during normal human activity and bad stress.

This book speaks against the bad or potentially destructive forms of stress flowing from work, relationships, health, and financial challenges rather than natural or good stressors such as exercise, excitement, and normal reactions to change and maturation.

Integrating Stress, Spirituality, and Personal Growth

There is a natural link between the way we respond to stress and our path of personal and spiritual growth. Stress and suffering are the surest paths to personal development because they place us squarely before human weakness and limitations. Both stressors and our response to them teach us about life and reveal where we need to grow.

This book is meant to facilitate dialogue with Jesus, who experiences, understands, and sympathizes with our trials; and with our neighbors, for we do not transform stress in isolation.

When we are knee-deep in stress and grief, it is difficult to pray, let alone to acknowledge the goodness of life and providence. When we don't feel God's presence and consolation, we can affirm the timeless complaint of Saint Teresa of Ávila: "If this is how You treat Your friends, it's no wonder You have so few of them."

Prayer is a battle. It is a suitable language and context for our reflections. It reflects our admission that we are dependent creatures who cannot make it by ourselves. Failure to recognize our need for God makes our stressors worse than they need to be.

A Way of Praying and Processing

Christian monastic tradition offers a holistic way of reflecting upon God's word. This way of reflection is known by its Latin name *lectio divina,* or "meditative reading or listening." *Lectio divina* can help us derive meaning and growth not only from written texts but from all types of personal experiences, especially stressful ones.

Lectio divina is well suited to our stress transformation objectives on two levels. First, it is a *whole-person process* for engaging a *whole-person challenge*. Second, what source is more intimately acquainted with stress and suffering than God's word? A model that helps us contemplate God's written word is suitable for pondering God's present word in our lives.

Lectio divina integrates human and divine values in a natural and accessible fashion. It provides a flexible framework and progression for individuals of all faiths who are trying to bring their lives in closer touch with God. In a personal enrichment culture bombarded on all sides with new theories and methods for personal growth, the oldest and simplest remains the most trustworthy.

The Path of *Lectio Divina*

Traditionally, *lectio divina* has been described as a natural progression of four stages: reading (or listening), meditation, prayer, and contemplation. To borrow the insight of Fr. Chester P. Michael, the steps can be summarized as reading, reflecting, responding, and resting. The implied fifth step, explicitly articulated in the Middle Ages, is *operatio*, or application in attitude and action.

From a human development perspective, the terms *active dialogue* and *receptive dialogue* (comprising the heartfelt expression of thoughts and emotions, and the listening, receptive state of silent presence) also describes the activity engaged in during the prayer and contemplation stages. *Lectio divina* describes the process of absorbing, analyzing, affecting, accepting, assimilating, and acting in response to a meaningful stimulus, in this case the stressors, challenges, and circumstances of your life.

In practice, reading to stimulate personal growth differs from studying, speed reading, or pleasure reading. It is done at a slower, more reflective pace, and in a holistic manner. We can create a comfortable physical, emotional, and spiritual space for prayerful reflection by finding a time and a location that are relatively peaceful and free of distractions.

Take each meditation by itself and linger over (and occasionally return to) those that strike a chord. You can take one line, thought, or image and return to it at various times during the day. As in any discipline, practice and repetition make perfect, or in our case, wholeness.

If your reflection leads to a more personal or authoritative source, such as the Bible, a favorite book or passage, an important memory, or your personal journal, pursue it. The meditations can serve as a stimulus for the interaction of your spirit with the Holy Spirit.

Lectio divina and spiritual discernment have great relevance in stress transformation. How can we make prudent decisions under pressure if we do not bring our whole selves into contact with the Holy Spirit? Dialoguing with God and our hearts is much healthier than worrying or engaging in endless analysis.

Resources on *lectio divina* can be found in the bibliography that follows the meditations.

Who This Book Is For

Although the personal growth and stress transformation focus of this book gives it a universal flavor, it should be of particular interest to individuals in highly stressful fields such as caregiving, counseling, pastoral care, chaplaincy, and Christian formation. The book can be used to nurture and guide others as well. Professionals in business and the trades may find it refreshing because of its relevance to a variety of real-world situations and its lack of technical jargon.

How to Use This Book

The meditations in this book, read in the spirit of *lectio divina,* can serve as daily quiet-time material or as thoughts for beginning or ending the day. Although the meditations are presented with a certain progression in mind, the topics stand on their own and can be pondered interchangeably.

Each topic begins with a thought from the Bible or Christian tradition. The meditation continues with a reflection that discusses how that particular topic can help us transform stress. Reflection questions clarify our feelings, attitudes, and experiences. Suggested action responses conclude each meditation by encouraging us to act in some small but efficacious way. These "little things" can make a big difference in stressful circumstances.

The meditations are also suitable for group settings—sharing, brainstorming, and feedback can inject objectivity and empathy into the growth process. Where group support is unavailable, individuals may wish to share personal reflections with a loved one or confidant. Stress has both individual and communal roots, and thus should be dealt with on both levels.

Space is provided at the end of most topics for you to record additional stress transformers, inspirations, and experiences. You can make this a personal or paschal journal.

A Note from the Author

As director of the Genesis Personal Development Center, I value and encourage feedback from readers of this book. To contact me directly, or to receive additional information about the center and its workshops and publications on time management, organizational development, male-female relationships, *lectio divina*, and the stress transformation and job therapy program, please use the address or phone number below.

Karl A. Schultz
Genesis Personal Development Center
3431 Gass Avenue
Pittsburgh, PA 15212
412-766-7545

Reflections on

Being
and
Doing

◆ ◆ ◆

We begin our meditations with the fundamental attitudes and perspectives that enable us to transform stress in cooperation with God, others, nature, and our true selves. These ideals and virtues are found not only throughout the Bible and Christian tradition but also in the consciousness of humanity.

The values and action responses proposed are commonplace and intuitive, with origins in our experience and heart. We may wonder how we have gotten away from them.

These timeless principles and practices help us discover our challenge and God's hand in facing the crosses we daily experience en route to the resurrection.

1

◆◆◆

Affirmation

Indeed, the word of God is living and active, sharper than any two-edged sword, piercing until it divides soul from spirit, joints from marrow; it is able to judge the thoughts and intentions of the heart. And before him no creature is hidden, but all are naked and laid bare to the eyes of the one to whom we must render an account. (Hebrews 4:12–13)

Therefore encourage one another and build up each other, as indeed you are doing. (1 Thessalonians 5:11)

The cynicism and moral corruption rampant in the modern world call for a radical practical remedy. We need a natural and inspired injection of encouragement and hope that can permeate the whole person. We are so bombarded with destructive influences that we must foster an alternative, and not just an empty house susceptible to even greater demons (see Luke 11:24–26).

Affirmation has two meanings. The first is the practice of internalizing a positive statement, image, or goal through periodic repetition. *Lectio divina* employs the principle of affirmation through the gentle, repetitive meditating, murmuring, or whispering of a meaningful or inspired verse, word, or phrase. The second meaning of affirmation is the active encouragement of ourselves or others through explicit recognition or rewards.

In practice these two meanings of affirmation complement each other. We need encouragement both internally and externally. Encouraging others reduces our stress by taking the focus off ourselves and increasing the possibility of reciprocal encouragement. We create a positive cycle of building up the human person and releasing the stressful toxins that come from isolation and extreme individualism.

The objective is to replace false and destructive images and beliefs that have permeated our conscious and subconscious mind with positive images and inspirations, and thereby to influence our behavior and choices. Affirmations become even more authoritative and influential when they are rooted in God's word. Scripture is the source par excellence of affirmations. Deep down we are more likely to doubt our word than God's word, though both have their own integrity and application.

Reflection Questions

◇ I would like to affirm or nurture myself in the following ways:
  ◇ mentally (caring for and building up the mind, self-image, and so on)
  ◇ spiritually (through reflection, meditation, prayer, spiritual reading, a retreat, a workshop, and so on)
  ◇ bodily (for example, through a physical or sensate activity: a good meal, a walk in the park, a relaxing bath)
◇ What affirmations would I like to internalize through periodic repetition? (Note: Remember to keep them brief, heartfelt, and positive. Words or images from the Bible and Christian tradition, as well as heartfelt affirmations born of experience and contemplation, can be especially persuasive to the subconscious mind because of their inherent authority and inspired source.)
◇ Do I talk negatively to myself in ways that pull me down? What are the roots of this destructive self-criticism? How can I change my self-talk to be more positive?

Action Responses

◇ Select a life or work area in which you will be particularly diligent in taking the opportunity to affirm yourself or others.
◇ Go out of your way to affirm a deserving person, especially if such affirmation will be unexpected.

2

◆◆◆

Prayer

> If you then, who are evil, know how to give good gifts to your children, how much more will the heavenly Father give the Holy Spirit to those who ask him! (Luke 11:13)

If God is our primary stress transformation helper, we should keep in constant touch with him. Prayer should not be confined to periodic quiet times and communal worship. It must be an ongoing dialogue with God as we work together to cope with and transform our circumstances.

Our prayer can take many forms. No one would deny the importance of praise, thanksgiving, and petition. Praise and thanksgiving take the focus off ourselves and give us a sense of peace. Petition enables us to throw our cares and concerns on God in hope of a response. But what about lament, the most popular prayer form in the Psalter?

We may initially recoil at the prospect of taking God to task through prayers of lamentation. However, just as a marriage is nourished through continual and honest communication, so is our relationship with God. Jesus' agony in the garden and his dying invocation of Psalm 22:2, "My God, my God, why have you forsaken me?" testifies that even God found the human condition overwhelming at times. If Jesus had difficulty with suffering, and brought his pain and fear to God, we would be arrogant to presume that we are above this. Lament helps us to get potentially toxic thoughts and emotions out of our system and into God's realm, where God can deal with them more effectively than either we or our neighbor can.

If God is our partner in transforming stress, we need to keep him apprised of how we are feeling, as much for our sake as for God's. God can handle whatever we give him. It's what we fail or refuse to give to God that creates our most serious problems.

Reflection Questions

◇ Do I bring my whole range of emotions and experiences before God, not just during quiet and worship times but as I go through the day?

◇ Do I believe that God loves me enough to accept my weaknesses as well as my strengths?

◇ Do I pay attention to God's initiative in my life on a daily basis?

◇ Do I believe that God cares enough to be involved with me in a mysterious way?

Action Responses

◇ Talk to God instead of fretting. Lament instead of whining. Pray your anger and anxiety instead of projecting them internally or externally onto others.

◇ View life and daily events as opportunities for prayer and greater intimacy with God and others.

3

◆◆◆

Silence

He said, "Go out and stand on the mountain before the LORD, for the LORD is about to pass by." Now there was a great wind, so strong that it was splitting mountains and breaking rocks in pieces before the LORD, but the LORD was not in the wind; and after the wind an earthquake, but the LORD was not in the earthquake; and after the earthquake a fire, but the LORD was not in the fire; and after the fire a sound of sheer silence. When Elijah heard it, he wrapped his face in his mantle and went out and stood at the entrance of the cave. (1 Kings 19:11–13)

In our lives we are rarely at a loss for noise. There is no shortage of words and images blaring at us. Unless we recognize this and carve out times of silence, this constant bombardment will make us tense and uptight. The littlest things will set us off. This chronic source of stress can impede our health and peace of mind.

Silence is a mode for encountering the roots of stress and depression. Do we periodically set aside time (even three minutes) to listen to the stirring of our hearts and to take internal inventory? Do we periodically permit ourselves to just "be" and rest in God's and life's presence?

If we are not in touch with our inner selves, how can we relate fully to others? We will be too busy resolving hidden conflicts that could have been unmasked and exposed had we taken the time to listen. In silence we exercise the gift of time to listen to our hearts and discern what God and life are calling us to in the present moment.

Slow me down, Lord. May I not be so noisy and hurried that I fail to experience what you, nature, and my loved ones communicate in silence.

Reflection Questions

◇ Why would I spend quality time in silence? What would be my objective?
◇ Do I have a time of day and an environment conducive to slowing down and listening?
◇ Do I occasionally step back and notice the sounds around me? What do I hear? Do I take for granted the sense of hearing?

Action Responses

◇ Experience silence in your life through daily quiet moments that help you center yourself and regain composure.
◇ Experience the silence that underlies the sounds of nature. Take periodic rejuvenating trips to elements of nature that speak to you: the ocean, lakes, woods, mountains. Let the environment slow you down to where you can listen to God and your heart, and discover a still point.

4

◆◆◆

Counsel

Fools think their own way is right,
   but the wise listen to advice.

(Proverbs 12:15)

The last thing we need in the midst of stressful times is isolation.
Because we don't have all the answers, we need the support and
wisdom of others. This does not imply that we should swing on the
whims and free advice of others; rather, it means we should seek out
and listen to those who measure their words carefully, who do not
provide easy answers, and who listen before they judge.

A trusted adviser provides us with objectivity. Although everyone
in their own way has wisdom to offer, we should have few confidants.
It can be very confusing and stressful, as well as time-consuming,
to find the truth amid a plethora of opinions. Having multiple coun-
selors can be as counterproductive as relying exclusively on our own
counsel.

In the midst of seeking external advice, do not forget to listen to
God and your heart.

Reflection Questions

◇ Do I have any burdens, large or small, on my heart that I wish to
   unload?
◇ Do I have anyone to whom I can go when I need to talk?
◇ In most situations do I rely solely on my own counsel, or do I
   prudently open myself to the wisdom of others?

Action Responses

◇ Find a support person, group, or service that you can benefit from on a periodic basis.

◇ Be a comforter or sounding board for a family member, friend, or peer.

5

◆ ◆ ◆

Anger

Those with good sense are slow to anger,
and it is their glory to overlook an offense.

(Proverbs 19:11)

Anger holds great potential for evil or for good. The challenge is to understand our anger and to channel it prudently. We should seek constructive ways of releasing intense emotions and energies. Such outlets include exercise, therapeutic counsel or support groups, dialogues with God, journaling, or a hobby.

Righteous anger can motivate us to bring good out of a negative situation. For example, it could lead us to forgive someone who has offended us; it could cause us to increase our efforts to reach a worthy goal that we have been denied unjustly.

The tragedy of Cain gives us precious insights into the stressful consequences of anger. When not expressed constructively to God or others, anger grows in intensity and irrationality and makes our face fall. Depression can be anger turned inward. Once we act improperly on our anger, we create greater problems for ourselves.

God initiated a dialogue with Cain to apprise him of the possibility of overcoming the inner urges and external temptations that sought to devour him (see Genesis 4:7; 1 Peter 5:8). God will engage in a similar dialogue and support faculty with us. It is important that we respond to this initiative by praying with our whole selves in moments of temptation (see Luke 22:40–44).

We too can master the intemperate and violent urges about which God warned Cain. By following the biblical principle and Christ's example of leaving vengeance and judgment to God, we save everyone much time and stress.

Reflection Questions

◇ What typical occurrences of anger do I need to look at and convert to constructive energy and action?
◇ What might be some roots of chronic or simmering anger?
◇ What preventive measures can I take to avoid anger-evoking situations?

Action Responses

◇ If communication and other attempts at conciliation fail, eliminate or limit your time with persons who consistently incite or frustrate you.
◇ Find constructive physical (exercise), emotional (counsel, journaling), and spiritual (spiritual direction and prayer) outlets for your anger, and affirm or reward yourself when you use them.

6

Coping
with
Criticism

It is better to hear the rebuke of the wise
than to hear the song of fools.

(Ecclesiastes 7:5)

Criticism originally meant "to get at the roots or essence of something." It had neutral connotations. Biblical or literary criticism, for example, is an attempt to extract and explore the underlying meaning of the object of review.

The form, tone, and content of the criticism we receive are often distorted. Where encouragement and guidance are needed, reprimands are given, and where firm correction is needed, feedback is withheld. Often we respond by perpetuating the cycle of negativity and projecting these distortions deeper into ourselves and others. The communication process wears down, and tension and stress levels rise.

Few of us have been taught how to correct others in a healthy and constructive fashion. Thus we need to affirm ourselves and re-build confidence and positivity. We need to respond proactively to this reality for the sake of ourselves as well as others.

The roots of violence in families and friendships are often found in the inability to accept or dispense criticism in a loving manner. Conversely, it is difficult to act aggressively toward someone who is criticizing you constructively by correcting or advising you with tears of caring in their eyes and by hugging or touching you.

Criticism is stressful when we approach it from an accusatory and divisive perspective. It is empowering when we offer and receive criticism with prudence, sensitivity, and the best interests of everyone at heart.

Reflection Questions

◇ How do I respond to and dispense criticism? How does it affect my interactions with others? Does criticism reduce or induce stress?

◇ Do I hold on to criticism and form resentments rather than discern its truthfulness and applicability and then let it go? What are the roots and influences underlying my approach?

◇ Do I look for opportunities to affirm as much as to correct? Do I administer both affirmation and criticism with the goal of building up the individual and the community?

Action Responses

◇ The next time you administer criticism or correction, preface your remarks with physical or verbal affirmation so that the person is aware of your good intentions. When you are tempted to respond defensively to criticism, hear the person out first, and gather yourself before you respond.

◇ Remember that the goal of criticism is to get at the roots or essence of something. Before sharing a criticism, ask yourself whether you are projecting a personal or situational bias that clouds your objectivity and will likely lead to misunderstanding and conflict.

7

◆◆◆

Proportion

A little yeast leavens the whole batch of dough. (Galatians 5:9)

We often react to events in a disproportionate way. We take people or their actions too seriously and make them our problems. We take ourselves too seriously and magnify offenses and worries. We transform irritants into major debacles.

One of the fruits of maturation is the ability to respond to life in proper measure by giving things the attention and effort they deserve. We won't always dole out the precise dosage, but we can do our best and keep learning and improving.

The concept of materiality is essential to healthy living: How important is something? What degree of response does it merit? Is it worth the psychic energy we are giving it?

We have a finite amount of resources, and thus must pick and choose our battles. We can learn to let go of little things and move on. If after disproportionate effort we eventually resolve an immaterial situation, what have we gained?

Reflection Questions

◇ Do I typically respond disproportionately to certain persons? Do I typically respond disproportionately to certain events or situations?
◇ What steps can I take to respond more in accordance with the circumstances?
◇ Do I incessantly punish and chastise myself for minor mistakes or offenses rather than correct and learn from them and move on?

Action Responses

◇ Periodically observe your typical reactions to persons, events, and situations. Identify instances and patterns of disproportionate response, and explore the roots of your reaction. The next time a similar circumstance arises, try to apply your enlightened approach. Even little improvements are valuable.

◇ When you find yourself overheating over trivialities, step back and balance the benefits and costs of your intensity. In most cases the prudent solution will be to cool off and find a more proportionate response. Pick your battles.

8

◆◆◆

Perspective

The eye is the lamp of the body. So, if your eye is healthy, your whole body will be full of light; but if your eye is unhealthy, your whole body will be full of darkness. If then the light in you is darkness, how great is the darkness! (Matthew 6:22–23)

Perspective flows from perception. It instinctively affects our reactions. If we misread a person or situation, we will respond correctly to it only by luck. Refining our perspective affects the stressor at its source.

We work on our perspective by listening, observing, and assimilating. We open ourselves to learning and growing and expanding our horizons. We submit ourselves to good stimuli and environments, and soak in their wisdom and opportunities.

We exacerbate our experience of stress by losing or distorting our sense of perspective. Much avoidable stress results when we take things out of context and fail to consider the whole picture. On what aspects of our life have we lost perspective? What are some of the consequences of this loss?

The Bible is our primary source for a Christian perspective. The first four chapters of Genesis provide a foundation for understanding both the ideal and the real qualities of the primary human relationships: with God, ourselves, others, and the natural and material world. The roots of stress ultimately lie in disordered relationships, beginning with prideful human mistrust of God and the disobedience born of this.

Much avoidable stress comes from subconsciously adopting materialistic perspectives on life. Like a computer, our mind, heart, and body will reflect its input. May we learn to see, feel, and think according to the data of the Scriptures, tradition, and the living church.

Reflection Questions

◇ What are the sources of my perspective? These can include faith, family, friends, and society. Do I have trusty sources, and do I drink from these wells often?

◇ Do I have blind spots or shadows in which my perspective seems a bit off? What experiences and hurts may have accounted for these distortions? When others alert me to my blind spots, for we cannot usually see them ourselves, do I listen and respond?

◇ How might I correct my biases and skewed outlooks? How do I get more in focus?

Action Responses

◇ Practice taking a step back from perplexing situations and thinking things out with the whole picture in mind. Minutiae can distort our vision.

◇ Take time periodically to examine your perspective. Observe its effects on your life and relationships. Observe how others act prudently in pressurized situations, and elicit their wisdom.

9

◆ ◆ ◆

Awareness

Consider the lilies of the field, how they grow; they neither toil nor spin, yet I tell you, even Solomon in all his glory was not clothed like one of these. (Matthew 6:28–29)

We invite avoidable stress when we lose touch with our intuition and senses. We become so absorbed in and focused on certain pursuits that we cut ourselves off from competing stimuli. There is a fine line between concentration and commitment, on the one hand, and obsession, on the other.

Awareness is the state of receiving vibrations or communications from ourselves and our environment. It is being in touch with ourselves and life. One of its chief challenges is chaos. When life is chaotic, we close the ranks and lose touch with stimuli outside our circle of concern. We limit ourselves and waste opportunities.

How do we regain and refine our awareness? Through the simple staples of silence, nature, simplicity, and humility. There is no instant recipe or esoteric formula involved. Awareness is a state of mind and desire. It is a choice that forsakes enticing alternatives laden with hectic and ambitious possibilities.

We cannot run at breakneck speed and expect to remain in touch with ourselves and our environment. How can we be aware when we are preoccupied with narrow pursuits? Take a hike, go to a mountain stream, walk by the ocean, and slow down. If you can't get there physically, go to these or other centering spots in your mind.

Reflection Questions

◇ Do I spend time daily trying to reacquaint myself with my senses? Do I eat slowly enough to taste and enjoy my food (and in the process naturally eat less)? Do I move about slowly enough that I enjoy the scenery along the way? Do I appreciate the sensate beauty of others?

◇ Do I pay attention to signals from my body and environment?

◇ Have any of my pursuits become obsessive and all-encompassing?

Action Responses

◇ When you drive somewhere, observe nature and people.

◇ When you encounter someone, really pay attention to them and the environment.

10
◆◆◆
Discernment

Do not be conformed to this world, but be transformed by the renewing of your minds, so that you may discern what is the will of God—what is good and acceptable and perfect. (Romans 12:2)

Discernment is becoming a lost art in our society of immediate gratification. We bring stress on ourselves or exacerbate pressures by not stepping back and getting to the roots of issues. We satisfy ourselves with simplistic short-term solutions because we dread accepting the challenge of long-term remedies that may require us to change.

Even the word *discernment* is disappearing from common parlance. How often do we speak of discerning our involvement in relationships and activities? Instead we let others tell us what to do, even though they are not apprised of all aspects of our situation. We say that most of the answers to our problems lie inside ourselves, but we sure don't act like it.

We can avoid unnecessary occasions of stress by using our judgment and intuition, by listening to our gut feelings. How many times have I had a bad or uneasy feeling about something but then analyzed myself away from it? Usually I come to regret my rejection of initial instincts and impressions, especially if they are not fueled by misinformation, paranoia, or prejudice.

In our overly rational Western culture, we do plenty of aggressive thinking and analyzing. Too often this is at the expense of praying, sensing, listening, receiving, and intuiting. We are action-oriented, at the expense of receptivity.

The Spiritual Exercises and Rules for Discernment of Spirits, by Saint Ignatius, provides a solid foundation for discernment. Modern decision-making theory uses many of the same principles. Among the best of the popular disseminations of Ignatian discernment principles are the works by Thomas H. Green, SJ. See the bibliography for details.

Reflection Questions

◇ Do I allow sufficient time and space for discernment before making important decisions?

◇ Do I supplement individual discernment with interpersonal or group counsel?

◇ Do I observe a pattern of knee-jerk decisions that result in unnecessary stress?

Action Responses

◇ Make important decisions from a position of strength and inner peace. Don't let others or circumstances pressure you to decide before you are ready.

◇ Use a journal regularly or periodically as a sounding board and thought and emotion clarifier.

11

◆ ◆ ◆

Dialogue

Ask, and it will be given you; search, and you will find; knock, and the door will be opened for you. For everyone who asks receives, and everyone who searches finds, and for everyone who knocks, the door will be opened. (Matthew 7:7–8)

How much unnecessary stress we bring on ourselves by trying to go things alone and by failing to communicate! How much time, energy, and anguish we would save by sharing one another's burdens and seeking or offering assistance when necessary!

A spirit of dialogue connotes openness to what others have to offer. It implies a receptivity to and appreciation for their gifts and difficulties. We pre-empt many stressors by making ourselves available and approachable to others. We make the effort and initiative to enter into an interactive and mutually beneficial communication process.

Many times our stress comes from ignorance or lack of resources or capacities. Others may help us if we ask them. We have to be willing to engage in the give-and-take of communication and to risk rejection or misunderstandings. Sometimes simply talking about our stressors to another person can broaden our perspective and give us a more objective sense of proportion.

Reflection Questions

◇ When I am stressed, do I try to work through my stress in isolation or in community?

◇ Am I willing to work out disputes and misunderstandings with others rather than play control and manipulation games?

◇ Do I learn and apply the stress-transforming advice and examples of others?

Action Responses

◇ The next time you find yourself getting worked up over a situation, try to engage in a constructive dialogue with an appropriate party.

◇ Don't be afraid to admit you need help and cooperation. Others may not always reciprocate, but many will assist as well as admire you for your courage and humility.

12

◆◆◆

Common Sense

Do not slight the discourse of the sages,
   but busy yourself with their maxims;
because from them you will learn discipline
   and how to serve princes.

(Sirach 8:8)

Common sense can go a long way toward eliminating needless stressors. Unfortunately, just because something can be deduced by straightforward reasoning doesn't mean that we will assimilate and apply it correctly. We have to cultivate common sense as part of our education, just as we do textbook knowledge. Common sense is a synthesis of experience, intelligence, intuition, and an understanding of the human psychology and condition.

Lack of common sense is at the heart of many stressors; for example, failing to get transactions or understandings into writing, letting the same person or group burn us continually, believing the improbable from a questionable source, and taking shortcuts as if they were free of conditions and consequences.

An effective way of developing common sense is through osmosis. Interact with those who consistently display common sense. Watch the way they operate. Ask them for pointers.

The nice thing about common sense is that it is available to everyone. Its primary prerequisite is that we desire it enough to acquire it through awareness and openness to knowledge and experience. Each day I can try to learn something new. So much of life is practical rather than theoretical knowledge. Common sense not only saves stress but time and energy as well. May we keep our eyes, ears, and minds open!

Reflection Questions

◇ Do I exercise poor judgment in some areas of my life? How might I remedy that through an injection of common sense? What resources can I draw upon?

◇ Do I know someone who seems to exercise good judgment and common sense in most situations? Try to meet with or observe them and let some of their prudence rub off.

◇ Do I emphasize book knowledge and intelligence at the expense of experience and common sense? Try to balance both.

Action Responses

◇ Practice common sense by engaging in transactions in which you have to rely partially on your judgment and intuition. Take modest risks that will pay off in valuable experience.

◇ Note the attributes held in common by persons who are skilled in everyday transactions and encounters. Apply some of these to your situation. Elderly folks have a storehouse of common sense ready to be tapped. Don't overlook them as a resource and support system.

13

◆◆◆

Tolerance

> But take care that this liberty of yours does not somehow become a stumbling block to the weak. (1 Corinthians 8:9)

We exacerbate situations and stressors by leaving little margin for error. It is prudent and charitable to give ourselves and others the benefit of the doubt. If we jump on every mistake, we'll wear ourselves and others out. Getting upset at every trifle or offense is a recipe for anxiety.

It is so much easier and effective to work with someone who will let you be human. Tolerance heads off unnecessary strains and conflicts. By being tolerant of others, we often receive tolerance in return. Further, unless we have been conditioned to be overly self-critical, we will naturally extend this same tolerance to ourselves.

Tolerance is not permissiveness. It simply gives people leeway to be human. We would want this extended to ourselves as well.

Reflection Questions

◇ How do I feel when I exercise tolerance toward others? toward myself? What are the typical practical results?

◇ Do I seem to be less tolerant in certain areas? What might be the reason for my intolerance, and what can I do about it?

◇ Conversely, am I excessively tolerant in certain areas? What corrections can I make to be more appropriately firm?

Action Responses

◇ Try to be more accepting of the foibles of family members. Think of the time and energy this saves!

◇ When you are tempted to give yourself a whipping over a minor indiscretion, remember the principle of tolerance—let it go and move on. Concentrate instead on solutions and possibilities. Such positivity is contagious!

14

◆◆◆

Ordered
Sensuality

"All things are lawful for me," but not all things are beneficial. "All things are lawful for me," but I will not be dominated by anything. (1 Corinthians 6:12)

Our culture overstimulates us sensually, enticing us to act imprudently and selfishly, then cautions us ominously about the consequences. Materialistic and hedonistic cultures promote unhealthy sensual values and stimuli.

Unrestrained or misdirected sensuality sooner or later creates stress for everyone. Because the attraction of sensuality is strong, we must fight it with a positive alternative as well as with self-control. We can't just say no. We have to say yes to something purer.

It is helpful to examine our attitudes about sexuality and the human body. If we view these as inherently bad, we will empower disordered conscious and subconscious tensions that may overpower us. Perhaps worse, we will deprive ourselves of a gift of God and one of the spices of life.

Sexuality and the body have boundaries and inherent principles that must be respected. Although observing these parameters brings its own pressures and stressors, they are minor compared to the consequences of uninhibited sensuality. Trying to subject our sensuality to reason and obedience yields healthy, if frustrating, stress, along with other virtues. Instinctively going with the flow at the expense of our conscience creates deeper stressors on both a moral and a practical plane.

Channeling our sensuality facilitates growth and good relationships. We accept the short-term stress this entails as a trade-off to the serious costs that a libertine lifestyle eventually brings.

Reflection Questions

◇ Do certain stimuli bring out my sensuality in a destructive way? Once I identify them, I can pursue an alternative outlet for constructive expression of my sensuality.

◇ Do my peers and relationships help or hinder my sensual attitudes and actions? Find an environment that helps rather than obstructs your progress.

◇ How does my positive and negative handling of my sensual capacities affect my stress level? Reflect on specific examples, and use them for motivation.

Action Responses

◇ Try to find healthy outlets and environments for sensual expression. Sensuality is good when used within the natural and divine laws. We want to avoid atrophy as well as anarchy.

◇ Read credible and time-tested literature on sexual topics rather than trendy material.

15

◆◆◆

Simplicity

Of course, there is great gain in godliness combined with contentment; for we brought nothing into the world, so that we can take nothing out of it; but if we have food and clothing, we will be content with these. But those who want to be rich fall into temptation and are trapped by many senseless and harmful desires that plunge people into ruin and destruction. For the love of money is a root of all kinds of evil, and in their eagerness to be rich some have wandered away from the faith and pierced themselves with many pains. (1 Timothy 6:6–10)

Nowadays almost everyone complains about being pressed for time and being in a hurry. Yet few us of are concerned, confident, and disciplined enough to make changes that will enable us to slow down.

Where are we going at the speed of light such that we are blinded to our environment and a blur to others? What is so important that we continually exhaust ourselves in the process? We "hurry-warts" ought to speak with a young wife whose husband is dying of cancer, or with parents whose child has a terminal illness. These people have learned about pace and priorities the hard way. They are a witness to the rest of us.

Hustle-bustle is a choice. Although certain activities and demands cannot be avoided without detrimental consequences for ourselves or others, we retain a substantial amount of control over the intensity and complexity of our lives. We can untangle ourselves from excess activities and commitments. Our schedule has play and flexibility that can be explored and managed according to our priorities. We can identify and redirect these discretionary activities if we are willing to take an honest look at our lives and discipline ourselves in certain areas.

Simplicity goes against the grain of our consumption-oriented and individualistic society. Simplicity strips away clutter and brings us into contact with the essentials of life. Perhaps we're afraid of what we might discover about ourselves, God, or life.

God, help us to recognize our limited nature and accept the grace and manageable possibilities and sufficient resources you provide in the present.

Reflection Questions

◇ What superfluous activities, possessions, commitments, rituals, and other energy drainers can I modify or eliminate?
◇ What areas of my life have gotten too complicated?
◇ What do I discover when I simplify my life?

Action Responses

◇ Try to discover and actualize manageable and healthy ways for simplifying your lifestyle and unloading excess baggage. Keep your eyes open on a daily basis for some action, routine, attitude, or communication that would profit from simplification.
◇ Before you make a major commitment of time, money, or energy, do a simple cost-benefit analysis, factoring in the spiritual and moral dimensions.

16

◆ ◆ ◆

Shabbat

> For in six days the LORD made heaven and earth, the sea, and all
> that is in them, but rested the seventh day; therefore the LORD
> blessed the Sabbath day and consecrated it. (Exodus 20:11)

I titled this meditation with the Hebrew verb *shabbat,* which means
"to rest," in appreciation of the fine tradition and example of Sabbath
observance offered by Jews. *Shabbat* encompasses a spirit and dis-
position, not just a rote observance. On a practical level, Christian
practice seems to have lost this.

One of the major reasons for our individual and collective stress is
that we exclude God from daily human affairs. Our loss of a Sabbath
sense is representative of this. Consider the societal and familial
effects of the repeal of the blue laws regarding commerce on the
Christian Sabbath, and the transformation of attitudes and lifestyles
that accompanied it. Even if we don't abide by this dishonoring of the
Sabbath, it affects us in our work and families. We face tremendous
pressure to go with the flow.

Human beings need a day dedicated to God and themselves.
We're not made to work seven days a week. The rest of the week is
devoted to exercising dominion over creation.

Why do we reject such a healthy, dignifying, even prestigious
idea? Because it is not productive according to materialistic values.
It doesn't build lopsided power and wealth. It recognizes our depen-
dence on God. It detracts from our selfish pursuits even as it refreshes
and delights us.

The *shabbat* spirit should not be confined to one day a week.
We should look for daily *shabbat* moments of rest and reorientation.
It's a natural mode of therapy, stress transformation, centering, and
empowerment.

Reflection Questions

◇ Can I find a pocket of time on the Sabbath as well as daily to discipline myself and influence my family members to slow down, rest, and rediscover God's love and providence?

◇ What activities or attitudes impede my Sabbath rest? What can I do about them?

◇ What are some wholesome, holy, and re-creational things I can experience on the Sabbath?

Action Responses

◇ Build Sabbath rest and daily *shabbat* moments into your schedule. Encourage others to do the same when they come to you looking for stress relief. Observe how you feel when the workweek starts after you have had your Sabbath rest. Read Abraham Joshua Heschel's classic text *The Sabbath*.

◇ If you can't eliminate certain tasks and responsibilities on the Sabbath (obviously, parental, filial, health care, and emergency service responsibilities are not suspended on the Sabbath), postpone the more intense and draining activities, and engage in potentially enjoyable and relaxing tasks.

17

◆ ◆ ◆

Gratitude

On the way to Jerusalem Jesus was going through the region between Samaria and Galilee. As he entered a village, ten lepers approached him. Keeping their distance, they called out, saying, "Jesus, Master, have mercy on us!" When he saw them, he said to them, "Go and show yourselves to the priests." And as they went, they were made clean. Then one of them, when he saw that he was healed, turned back, praising God with a loud voice. He prostrated himself at Jesus' feet and thanked him. And he was a Samaritan. Then Jesus asked, "Were not ten made clean? But the other nine, where are they? Was none of them found to return and give praise to God except this foreigner?" Then he said to him, "Get up and go on your way; your faith has made you well." (Luke 17:11–19)

It is easier to complain about our lack than to appreciate and work with our bounty. Such complaining creates stress rather than peace and solutions. Even in times of exceptional suffering and stress, each of us can discover gifts and blessings that we have taken for granted. Very often they are right in front of our nose: loved ones, health, hobbies or favorite activities, talents, skills, and opportunities. We should appreciate them because there is no guarantee they will be there tomorrow.

We can find much to be thankful for if we are willing to humble ourselves and open our eyes and heart to God's generosity. We are much happier when we content ourselves with the gifts we possess at the present moment rather than bemoan what could or should have been.

Gratitude is a juncture of spirituality and human wisdom: it compels us to trust God and accept what we have. It is amazing how few material essentials there really are.

Reflection Questions

◇ Who am I grateful for? What experiences or memories am I grateful for? Why?

◇ What events, circumstances, or opportunities am I grateful for? What skills and talents am I grateful for? Why?

◇ What hobbies or activities am I grateful for? What material possessions or wealth am I grateful for? Why?

Action Responses

◇ Look for things to be thankful to God and others for on a daily basis. Express your gratitude toward someone who extends a kindness to you that you might normally take for granted. See how much more peaceful and less stressed you feel.

◇ In the midst of a bad day, recall some of the things you can be thankful for. Watch your mood, perspective, and behavior change.

18

◆ ◆ ◆

Generosity
and
Detachment

If one is mean to himself, to whom will he be generous?
    He will not enjoy his own riches.
No one is worse than one who is grudging to himself;
    this is the punishment for his meanness.
If ever he does good, it is by mistake;
    and in the end he reveals his meanness.

(Sirach 14:5–7)

Generosity and detachment are becoming lost virtues in Western culture. With the climate of mistrust, self-seeking, and possessiveness that permeates our social and economic environments, it is not surprising that we get attached to spiritual, material, and emotional entities and turn them into crutches or idols. It is difficult for us to let go not only of possessions, wealth, and power but also of persons, circumstances, and routines that give us pleasure and security.

We can become so enamored and dependent on these entities that we become their slaves. Generosity takes the focus off ourselves through the act of giving. Such selfless giving goes against both our natural and conditioned tendencies, but it brings out the best in ourselves, others, and our environment.

Generosity and detachment are liberating virtues that remind us that we possess things and experience persons or circumstances as gift; we will not have them in this world forever. We gain perspective on our stressors and God's gifts when we reach out to others by giving of ourselves.

Our outreach will not always reward us with a warm-fuzzy feeling. Others can be oblivious or ungrateful. Sometimes we'll make mistakes in the process of giving. Our reaction to rejection reveals how close to the spirit of Christ we are (see Luke 9:51–56). In Luke 17:10, Jesus testifies to the gratuitous spirit that should underlie our service: "So you also, when you have done all that you were ordered to do, say, 'We are worthless slaves; we have done only what we ought to have done!'"

Reflection Questions

◇ To whom, including myself, do I wish to be more generous? In what circumstances can I be more generous?
◇ Why am I not as generous as I could be?
◇ What physical, emotional, or material entities do I cling to in an unhealthy manner?

Action Responses

◇ Look for small steps you can take to appreciate and share God's gifts without clinging to them.
◇ Try to give without expecting recompense or reward, especially with loved ones. Try to build your happiness on lasting values and relationships rather than on transient ones.

19

◆ ◆ ◆

Peacemaking

A soft answer turns away wrath,
  but a harsh word stirs up anger.

(Proverbs 15:1)

Western culture thrives on competition and division. Media and entertainment institutions incite it. The church itself is beset by factions and divisions. Reconciliation efforts do not grab the headlines, and usually receive funding only through political connections or media attention. If you want to be a peacemaker, you can find support groups and co-operative efforts, but you will be subject to rejection, derision, apathy, and aggression. People and the economy are stimulated by conflict and diversity.

Peacemaking begins in small ways. Avoid unnecessary arguments and confrontations. Act prudently in relationships. Omit provocative words, gestures, or behaviors.

I must work at peacemaking on several levels: with God, other persons, myself, and the material and natural world. I must first be at peace with myself.

Peace is not happiness or pleasure. You can feel lousy and still be at peace. Peace is not an escape from reality. The peace of Christ differs from the peace the world gives. Inner peace enables me to perceive and respond to stressors fluidly. Peacemaking may actually make our situation worse, but the benefits of a clean conscience and the peace we spread dwarf any circumstantial drawbacks. Peace can start with a smile, a small favor, an attitude of acceptance and conciliation.

Do I value and desire peace sufficiently to do what it takes to help reconcile even a small part of our divided world?

Reflection Questions

◇ What issues cause me the most chronic anxiety and lack of peace? What can I do about this?

◇ Which of my relationships or activities merit stepping up my peace-making activities?

◇ Am I at peace with myself? Why or why not? How can I be more at peace?

Action Responses

◇ Avoid getting into an argument with someone over an emotional topic. Instead of getting sucked in by the aggressiveness and insecurity of others, do not let them dictate your actions.

◇ Try to be a peacemaker with at least one person you encounter each day. A gesture as simple as a smile, handshake, or kind word can get you started on the right foot.

20

◆◆◆

Fiscal Prudence

Keep your lives free from the love of money, and be content with what you have; for he has said, "I will never leave you or forsake you." So we can say with confidence,

"The Lord is my helper;
I will not be afraid.
What can anyone do to me?"

(Hebrews 13:5–6)

Money is often at the root of our anxiety. Handling money and other resources is a difficult challenge that can be aided by simple logic, planning, and self-discipline. For example, carrying credit cards with large unpaid balances does not make financial sense.

It is truly amazing how far money can go when it is carefully monitored. It is equally amazing how fast it can go when we are lax in managing it.

Assuming we are cutting out luxuries as opposed to necessities, we can use our creativity to inject fun into the process. Sit down, compare your projected revenues and expenses, identify dispensable expenditures, and carve out a cushion for emergency and discretionary expenditures such as rewarding ourselves for good money management.

Some of the best things in life are free or affordable. As painful as it may be at times, and as much as we would prefer the luxury of significant cash and material reserves, fiscal prudence can build character and foster enrichment through the exercise of our imagination and resourcefulness.

Reflection Questions

◇ What steps can I take to economize through simple planning and self-discipline?
◇ Who do I know that can help me manage my finances better?
◇ What free or affordable activities are available to me?

Action Responses

◇ Implement some manageable and effective changes you can make in your budget or spending habits.
◇ Spend money for what you need and can afford. Be wary of expenditures whose primary attraction is as a good deal or a bargain. Our lives are full of "bargains" we never use.

21

◆ ◆ ◆

Humor

Feasts are made for laughter;
   wine gladdens life,
   and money meets every need.

(Ecclesiastes 10:19)

There are plenty of grim souls around. Most of us take ourselves and our circumstances too seriously, as if the whole world rests on our shoulders. Seriousness needs to be complemented by humor, which is the capacity to be amused and enthused by life and to share this capacity with others. Humor has no precise boundary or blueprint; each individual has a unique style, gifts, and opportunities.

One fun way to disarm stressors is to lighten up. Be appropriately silly and open to laughter. Inject a little levity into life.

Authentic humor never occurs at another's expense. Opportunities for humor flow from life itself and from our openness and creativity; if we wish to find things in life to laugh at, we will.

The absurdity of life must be good for some humor, especially because we humans do so many crazy things. Laughter and levity are good for the mind, body, and spirit. When enjoyed in moderation, they are a medicine without harmful side effects.

An interesting aspect of the Bible is that it rarely praises humor apart from its appropriateness in festive occasions. It seems to extol sobriety and even sorrow rather than mirth, especially in reference to this life (see, for example, Ecclesiastes 7:3–4). A closer look at the Beatitudes, however, reveals that part of the mystery of God's will is that the major thrust of our laughter will come in the Kingdom of God (see Luke 6:21).

The Bible is simply being true to reality; this world, despite its many joys and pleasures, can be a vale of tears. Some people seem to lead charmed lives, whereas others frequently get it in the neck. Jesus foretold that we would weep while the world rejoices (John 16:20–24).

Reflection Questions

◇ How can I take myself less seriously?

◇ How can I take the foibles and annoying habits of others (especially loved ones) less seriously?

◇ How can I take the ups and downs of life more evenly?

Action Responses

◇ Work on aspects of your personality or perspective that need an injection of humor or playfulness (for example, things you seem to overreact to or take too seriously).

◇ Try to respond gracefully to everyday occurrences or situations that would normally ruffle your feathers. You can even try to find humor in them. It's better than getting stressed out! You make more friends that way.

22

◆◆◆

Acceptance

Then Job answered the LORD:
   "I know that you can do all things,
   and that no purpose of yours can be thwarted.
'Who is this that hides counsel without knowledge?'
Therefore I have uttered what I did not understand,
   things too wonderful for me, which I did not know.
'Hear, and I will speak;
   I will question you, and you declare to me.'
I had heard of you by the hearing of the ear,
   but now my eye sees you."

(Job 42:1–5)

In the context of suffering and stress, acceptance is a sensitive topic because it is always easier to speak about it than to live it. It is not the intellectual struggle that is so difficult but the submission of will.

Acceptance is constituted by two questions: Are we willing to let God have ultimate control of our lives without abdicating our human responsibilities? Are we willing to pray constantly and to depend actively on God's grace in fulfilling the first question? If we know that we are trying to live life as best we can, by God's grace we can learn to accept things and make the best of them. A clean conscience is a tremendous stress reducer and peace producer.

Fighting life is counterproductive. The best way to respond to difficult circumstances is first to accept that they are real, to affirm in faith that something good will come of the situation, and to take constructive steps, however small, to improve the situation. This rules out passively or irresponsibly caving in to opposition or standards that we feel are unjust.

We try to implement the Serenity Prayer, attributed to Reinhold Niebuhr, which profoundly and succinctly encompasses the challenge of acceptance: "God, give us grace to accept with serenity the things that cannot be changed, courage to change the things which should be changed, and the wisdom to distinguish the one from the other."

Reflection Questions

◇ In what areas of my life do I need to be more accepting?
◇ What aspects of my personality or background make me more or less accepting?
◇ What are the consequences to my health of the things I don't accept?

Action Responses

◇ Make minor action or attitude adjustments that will enable you to accept your current circumstances more peacefully.
◇ Make a point of accepting your own and others' shortcomings and strengths.

23

◆◆◆

Choosing
Our Company

Whoever walks with the wise becomes wise,
    but the companion of fools suffers harm.

(Proverbs 13:20)

Do not be deceived:
    "Bad company ruins good morals."

(1 Corinthians 15:33)

One of the worst ways to fight depression is to surround ourselves with chronic complainers, especially those who do little to improve their situation. Conversely, some of the best company to keep is that of individuals who have managed to maintain a cheerful attitude despite difficult circumstances. Their personal depth and demeanor can serve as an inspiration and model. They teach us that happiness is a choice and a gift, a by-product of integrity rather than something to be appropriated and possessed.

Jesus was careful in selecting his companions. He knew the sting of human treachery, betrayal, and abandonment from those closest to him. He wanted his followers to know what life with him required (see Luke 9:57–62). He knew the influence his followers would have on one another, as reflected most prominently in the Acts of the Apostles. We would do well to heed his words and ally ourselves with trustworthy companions.

Reflection Questions

◇ Are the people I keep company with depressing or uplifting?
◇ What attracts me to the individuals or peer groups with whom I associate?
◇ How am I influenced by my companions? What are the fruits of my friendships?

Action Responses

◇ Take a concrete step every day to improve the quality of your relationships, activities, or peer groups. This can be achieved through something as simple as a smile, a kind word, a favor, or a compliment.
◇ When your friends or peers involve themselves in activities or conversations that you know are wrong or wasteful, try to steer them to a positive alternative. If they won't join you, go yourself.

24

◆ ◆ ◆

Compassion
and
Service

> Truly I tell you, just as you did it to one of the least of these who are members of my family, you did it to me. (Matthew 25:40; see also Isaiah, chapter 58)

Serving persons who are suffering or who are less fortunate than ourselves is a powerful antidote to stress. We can then channel our energies in life-giving ways.

Such service does not need to be grand or extraordinary; small acts of kindness and courtesy such as a smile or a simple favor can do wonders for people, as Jesus pointed out: "Whoever gives even a cup of cold water to one of these little ones in the name of a disciple— truly I tell you, none of these will lose their reward" (Matthew 10:42).

Suffering and fellow sufferers teach us what is important in life. They help us to reconsider our priorities and reform our values. Caregivers who serve the poor marvel at the profound dignity and simple peacefulness of those who lack what we consider essential to happiness. Serving or spending time with people in pain takes the spotlight off our woes. Experiencing life with such persons helps us view our situation from a different viewpoint; our joys, sorrows, and anxieties are brought into perspective.

Reflection Questions

◇ To whom can I extend a kindness or a visit to show that I care? (Reminder: Do not overlook family or friends—charity begins at home.)
◇ Do I feel called to a particular service activity or project? Does this project fit within my time constraints and resources?
◇ Do I treat persons I meet on a daily basis with compassion and warmth? We never know what their secret sufferings are.

Action Responses

◇ Try each day to do a simple act of kindness or service for someone.
◇ Extend the same compassion and simple acts of kindness to yourself.

25

◆◆◆

Creativity

> When it was evening, the disciples came to him and said, "This is a deserted place, and the hour is now late; send the crowds away so that they may go into the villages and buy food for themselves." Jesus said to them, "They need not go away; you give them something to eat." They replied, "We have nothing here but five loaves and two fish." And he said, "Bring them here to me." (Matthew 14:15–18)

Although not all problems can be solved, we can usually find ways to make the best of a difficult situation. Necessity can bring out the best and most creative parts of ourselves. We can discover and develop latent gifts and strengths.

In most situations, we can take small, seemingly insignificant measures to improve the situation of ourselves or others. Using silence, counsel, and basic problem-solving tools such as brainstorming and making pro-and-con lists, we can use our imagination, intuition, and reasoning faculties to formulate an innovative response to our dilemma.

The Gospels are full of situations in which Jesus was confronted with an unexpected guest or request. It was up to him to heal and put people at ease. Spiritually speaking, creativity is participation in the creative initiative of God, who brings life out of chaos.

Reflection Questions

◇ Do I see myself as a creative person? Why or why not?
◇ If I used more of my creative potential, how might my attitude and experience of life be different?
◇ Do I approach difficult situations fatalistically, or with confidence and resourcefulness?

Action Responses

◇ Brainstorm small steps you can take to lessen your stress from a given problem or circumstance (for example, minor adjustments in outlook or behavior that will improve the situation and make the problem less debilitating).

◇ Acknowledge stalemate situations that might benefit from a different approach, and apply one.

26

◆ ◆ ◆

Humility

> In itself, humility is nothing else but a man's true understanding and awareness of himself as he really is. It is certain that if a man could truly see and be conscious of himself as he really is, he would indeed be truly humble. (Anonymous author of *The Cloud of Unknowing*)

Pride is an obstacle when we are feeling stressed. It can influence us to deny that we are depressed or in a rut. Pride can keep us from acknowledging that our emotional, spiritual, and practical reactions are uniquely ours.

Humility gives us the courage to say to ourselves: "This event or circumstance is largely outside of my control, but I do have control over my response. If I am partially responsible for my predicament, I can forgive myself, ask forgiveness of others, and go on from there. Despite my good intentions, I realize I fail in so many ways, both known and unknown. I can take responsibility for my attitude and actions and resolve to do my best. I may be, at least partially, a victim of circumstances, but I am not helpless."

Humility compels us to admit that we are weak persons who need help. We cannot thrive on an island of our own making. Humility inspires us to seek solutions that may dictate a modification of our attitudes or behavior patterns. Humility helps us to acknowledge both our achievements and our mistakes without dwelling on them. As Saint Augustine pointed out, human perfection is in finding out our own imperfection.

Reflection Questions

◇ How could humility help me make inroads on self-induced stress?
Does my pride sometimes exacerbate my stressors (for example,
an unwillingness to follow directions or act obediently)?
◇ Can I acknowledge some responsibility or need for assistance that
will relieve part of my burden?
◇ Do I invite stress by trying to do too much? If so, why and where?
What is my remedy for this?

Action Responses

◇ Let go of resentment over an unkind remark or offensive gesture
made by someone acting out of intensity or immaturity rather than
maliciousness. Accept criticism that is well intended but clumsily
offered. Apply what is helpful, and let go of the rest.
◇ Acknowledge, rectify, and forgive mistakes or shortcomings in your
areas of weakness and vulnerability.

27

◆◆◆

Living
in the
Present

So do not worry about tomorrow, for tomorrow will bring worries of its own. Today's trouble is enough for today. (Matthew 6:34)

A common cause of self-applied pressure is the refusal to live in the present. We can become loaded down with regret over the past or anxiety about the future. Yet reality is always in the present. The past is no more, and the future is not yet. Living in the present helps us to enjoy and optimize the current situation because we are participating in it more fully. We are present in mind, body, and spirit.

Living in the present distracts us from idle worry or speculation. The circumstances before us consume our energies and attention, and we do not have time to dwell on circumstances that could be or might have been, and over which we are helpless to affect change.

Living in the present is not a complicated process, but it does require awareness, self-discipline, and courage. Sometimes the present is painful, and it is easier to seek an escape. Yet the present is where healing and transformation occur. Healing of the past and preparation for the future occur in the present. Presence to the present is good spirituality and good psychology.

Jesus had more to worry about than anyone, but he waited until the moment of truth, Gethsemane, to deal with his fears. God provided him with strength when he needed it.

Let us pray for the grace to put one foot in front of the other, and to do in a spirit of trust and peace what seems appropriate in the present moment. Can anything be more simple and attainable, yet so challenging and fulfilling?

Reflection Questions

◇ Specifically, how can I be more present to persons and events?
◇ Am I living in the future or in the past? If so, why?
◇ What changes in attitude and perspective do I need to make to anchor myself in the present?

Action Responses

◇ In your daily interactions with loved ones, make a conscious, wholehearted effort to listen and to try to understand them.
◇ If you find a pattern of missing the present through preoccupation with other matters, address the distractions and return to the present.

28

◆◆◆

Patience
and
Perseverance

Have patience with everyone, but chiefly with yourself. (Saint Francis de Sales)

Anxiety and depression are evoked by our refusal to let the future come to us. We worry about things that exist only in our imagination, and find ourselves distracted from the task at hand. We want things to happen according to our timetable, but usually that is not the way life works.

Only with experience and maturity do we recognize that our timetable is not necessarily the best for everyone, including ourselves. We are better off maintaining a tempered position of doing our best and flowing with the rest. A common message of those who have made great strides in their profession or vocation is: "Eventually hard work pays off, but not necessarily the way you expect. Believe in yourself, and never stop trying. Patience and perseverance breed success through a gradual process of self-discipline and discernment."

According to James 5:11, Job is an outstanding model of perseverance. In the Book of Job, Job's patience lasts only two chapters. What is especially inspiring and comforting about Job is that he perseveres even when everyone, including God, seems to be against him. He believes in himself and refuses to compromise his integrity. Under highly stressful conditions, Job holds on to his dignity and is vindicated in the end for his honesty (see Job 42:7–10.

Sometimes we wish God would show pride in us (see Job, chapters 1 to 2) in a different way. Why did God wait until after Job's restoration to send him caregivers (see Job 42:11)? Where was Job's support system when he needed one?

In the spirit of Job, we should feel free to place our questions and feelings before God when our patience and perseverance are sorely tried. I sometimes take Job's lamentations and put them in my own words. This makes the word of God the basis for my prayer even when I don't feel like offering praise or thanksgiving. Sometimes the Spirit offers consolation and enables me to praise God in my own way for the little positive elements I can find, because things are never completely dark.

I am glad that God is gracious about our human complaints and frustrations. God, you preach truth, now you're going to get it from me! Help me to trust that you are in my darkness and desolation, and that you treasure and sustain my patience and perseverance.

Reflection Questions

◇ In what areas or specific instances do I need more patience and perseverance?
◇ Why do I persevere amid difficult circumstances?
◇ Am I patient with myself in most situations? Can I think of any exceptions or patterns?

Action Responses

◇ Pick an area or relationship in which you are typically impatient and work on being more patient.
◇ Give yourself a reward or affirmation for trying when you feel like quitting. Offer substantive encouragement or practical help to someone who is teetering under the pressure.

Reflections on
Lifestyle Issues
and
Activities

◆ ◆ ◆

Our reflections on being and doing provided us with a practical and conceptual framework for transforming stressors into growth. However, unless we implement these in our everyday life, they will remain pious platitudes and ineffectual ideals.

If we are attentive to these practical "staffs of life," we will naturally, rather than through force, find ourselves living a more whole and holy life. We will be so busy trying to image God in word and deed in the circumstances of life that we won't have the time or energy to concern or stress ourselves with what is beyond our capabilities.

> O LORD, my heart is not lifted up,
>   my eyes are not raised too high;
> I do not occupy myself with things
>   too great and too marvelous for me.
> But I have calmed and quieted my soul,
>   like a weaned child with its mother;
>   my soul is like the weaned child that is
>   with me.
>
> O Israel, hope in the LORD
>   from this time on and forevermore.
>   (Psalm 131:1–3)

29

◆◆◆

Music

David also commanded the chiefs of the Levites to appoint their kindred as the singers to play on musical instruments, on harps and lyres and cymbals, to raise loud sounds of joy. (1 Chronicles 15:16)

Music can be a tremendous aid in fighting depression and stress. Music with a positive message—either an objective universal message (due to uplifting lyrics and soothing melodies) or a subjective personal message (due to the memories and feelings it evokes)—can provide a welcome relief from the often inane programming of television and radio, and the bias and negativity of much of the print media.

Also, music does not require our attention to the extent that television and print media do. We can listen to music while working on certain things; carry on a conversation with light music in the background; exercise to it; use it to lull us to sleep; or listen to it attentively. Lying down and listening to a favorite piece of music with the lights turned off is an excellent way to clear the mind and relax after a busy day.

In a health-care and personal growth context, guided meditations accompanied by soothing music can be used to heal emotions and the subconscious mind. Many persons take up playing an instrument, singing, songwriting, or composing at least partly for therapeutic or communication purposes.

Adaptable to a variety of motivations, tastes, and resources, music is part of the seasons of an individual's life, from times of grieving and good-byes to celebrations and beginnings.

When I am angry, upset, or depressed, I play music that touches my heart. This may yield tears, and perhaps even intense emotions, but at least it stirs something in me.

Music has a way of giving us perspective. Music can remind us that life is too short to hold grudges and dwell on bitter memories of the past.

Reflection Questions

◇ What meaning or benefits does music offer me? Why do certain songs, artists, or styles of music speak to me?

◇ Do I listen to relaxing and inspiring music as much as I like? If not, what's stopping me?

◇ Do I use music to help me smile, relax, regain perspective, and reduce stress by stirring up positive memories and forgotten values?

Action Responses

◇ Make music a more integral and therapeutic part of your life by taking just twenty minutes to listen, relax, and settle yourself.

◇ Celebrate a moment, enjoy time with a loved one or friend, or reward yourself for sincere efforts by listening to your favorite album or artist, or perhaps by purchasing a desired title.

30

◆◆◆

Boredom Busters

Just as you do not know how the breath comes to the bones in the mother's womb, so you do not know the work of God, who makes everything.

In the morning sow your seed, and at evening do not let your hands be idle; for you do not know which will prosper, this or that, or whether both alike will be good. (Ecclesiastes 11:5–6)

Although boredom is sometimes unavoidable, such as during a long hospital stay, in most situations we can take diversionary measures to avoid boredom. The unique nature of individual preferences, circumstances, and resources prompts us to list the general possibilities open to us: hobbies, enjoyable activities, and other forms of recreation; social interactions and relationships; community activities; service projects; exercise; continuing education; professional or personal growth endeavors.

We don't usually think of boredom as stressful even though it can make us depressed or anxious. Boredom results when we lack meaningful and constructive activity.

Do not confuse purposeful activity, which can include recreational and therapeutic pursuits, with hyperactivity. Our objective is to achieve some degree of equilibrium between the extremes of boredom and hyperactivity. Both can be a flight from reality, and each has negative health consequences.

Boredom has a moral dimension in that excessive idleness can cause us to waste the creative potential God has given us. There is truth in the proverb, "Idle hands are the playthings of the devil."

Rather than approach the desired activity equilibrium from a negative or scrupulous perspective, why not brainstorm activities or goals we could be pursuing, within our capacity and means, that would build up others, the world, or ourselves? We do not necessarily need to look for major projects, but for something worthwhile that can get us started in the right direction. We can whip boredom one step at a time.

Reflection Questions

◇ What are my hobbies or recreational activities? What role does exercise or other physical activity play in my life?
◇ What social interactions and relationships are important to me? What community activities or service organizations might I begin or increase my involvement in?
◇ In what areas might I pursue continuing education? What are my personal growth or achievement goals?

Action Responses

◇ Do something constructive and stimulating to overcome feelings of boredom. Perhaps help someone else out of their doldrums.
◇ Participate in an activity that will get your creative, intellectual, spiritual, or social juices flowing.

31

◆◆◆

Rut Breakers

> The apostles gathered around Jesus, and told him all that they
> had done and taught. He said to them, "Come away to a deserted
> place all by yourselves and rest a while." (Mark 6:30–31)

In both ruts and boredom, we are not sufficiently using our creative
capacities. Both repetition and idleness anesthetize and understimu-
late us. We become antsy and listless. Ruts differ from boredom in that
we have something constructive to do, but the rituals and routines are
lulling us into sloppiness and lethargy. In the workplace, technology
often plays a role in the creation of ruts, along with an unbalanced
economy in which most of the available jobs are routine and low-
paying.

We can trust that ruts can be used for God's purposes, especially
when we cooperate by using wholesome means for rejuvenating our
creative energies and potential. Prayer is a good rut breaker because
it aids discernment and opens us to the creative inspiration of our
personal gifts and the Holy Spirit. If there is one thing that will neither
bore you nor put you in a rut, it's the action of the Holy Spirit. It may
drive you to wit's end, but at least life will have meaning and energy,
even if you don't understand the form and direction it takes.

Rut breakers all have a common objective: variety and deviation
from the norm. The formula is quite simple. If we are stuck in a rut, we
must do something different to pull ourselves out. We need to break
out of stifling patterns and routines. We temporarily remove ourselves
from our current situation, if not physically, then emotionally and
mentally, in order to gain greater objectivity and creative energy in
assessing and responding to it.

Consider local or distant travel as a rut-breaking possibility. A
change of scenery can be helpful. Recreation and relaxation are
great vehicles for breaking a rut. Pursue an activity that you enjoy and
perhaps have neglected lately. Break the self-imposed bonds that impede a healthy and effective response to your present circumstances.

Concurrent with external efforts, take constructive measures to regain your interior freedom and motivation. Get "unstuck" by transforming a negative attitude or situation into a positive alternative. Achieve little victories by doing whatever you can to overcome stagnancy by purposeful change and variation.

Reflection Questions

◇ What stimulating or diversionary activities would I like to pursue?
◇ Where might I go? How about a change of pace or scenery, however slight?
◇ With whom would I be re-energized by spending time together?

Action Responses

◇ Brainstorm simple, nonspectacular things you can do on a daily basis to break from the norm and add spice to the day.
◇ When you are in a rut, take the risk of asking for assistance or inspiration. When you find someone else in a rut, help them out.

Reflections on
Moderation
and
Balance

◆ ◆ ◆

The Latin expression, *"virtu stat in medium,"* states that virtue stands in the middle. Most religions and philosophies ascribe to this truth. Although we know this intuitively and rationally, arriving at a healthy medium in practical circumstances is another matter.

Any constructive personal or family growth endeavor must embrace the virtues of moderation and balance, and respect their boundaries and guidelines. In this section we will focus on five practical lifestyle areas (sleep, work and play, diet, exercise, and family) and the foundational elements of moral tension (prohibition versus scrupulosity, permission versus permissiveness) in which humans are tempted to go to extremes.

Although one could devote entire books to each topic, consider these brief reflections as a reminder and a catalyst. It is good to consider periodically how well we are balancing the basics and taking care of ourselves and our loved ones.

32

◆◆◆

Sleep

How ample a little is for a well-disciplined person!
    He does not breathe heavily when in bed.
Healthy sleep depends on moderate eating;
    he rises early, and feels fit.
The distress of sleeplessness and of nausea
    and colic are with the glutton.
If you are overstuffed with food,
    get up to vomit, and you will have relief.
Listen to me, my child, and do not disregard me,
    and in the end you will appreciate my words.
In everything you do be moderate,
    and no sickness will overtake you.

(Sirach 31:19–22)

The December 17, 1990 issue of *Time* magazine brought to popular attention what specialists have known for years: Americans are not getting enough sleep. The reasoning justifying this deficiency is circular: We don't have enough time to get proper rest, so we neglect it in favor of functioning inefficiently and uncomfortably. We feel lousy while we take more time to get less done and then complain that we're too busy.

During times of crisis and transition, sleep loss and irregular sleeping patterns may be unavoidable. Individuals require different amounts of sleep. You can determine this through self-observation and consultation with your doctor.

Proper amounts of sleep give us a healthy foundation for coping with stress and daily challenges. Lack of sleep can reduce alertness and energy levels, and lead to irritability and depression. That is a significant price to pay for the time we borrow from sleep.

What could be sillier than worrying when we should be sleeping, and sleeping when we should be working or playing? Why not wake up in the morning with more energy and fewer cobwebs? Make the schedule, behavior pattern, and lifestyle changes conducive to getting proper rest. We're no good to anybody when we're chronically tired.

Reflection Questions

◇ How many hours of sleep do I need to wake up refreshed? How many hours have I been getting? If applicable, consider why there is a disparity and what can be done about it.
◇ Do I think that there may be psychological or moral factors underlying my erratic sleeping patterns that merit consultation with a therapist or spiritual director?
◇ Am I willing to make the financial, social, lifestyle, or professional sacrifices necessary to get proper rest and sleep? Am I willing to monitor my lifestyle and activities so that I can operate within time and resource constraints? If my answers are yes, what obstacles might I face, and how will I respond to them?

Action Responses

◇ If you would like to increase or decrease your amount of sleep, set a goal and work toward it. Record practical steps you will take to achieve it. When you begin to achieve a stable pattern and sufficient level of sleep, affirm yourself and note any observable benefits or by-products.
◇ Slow down your pace in the evening before going to bed. This makes a better transition to sleep.

33

♦♦♦

Work
and
Play

> There is nothing better for mortals than to eat and drink, and find
> enjoyment in their toil. This also, I saw, is from the hand of God;
> for apart from him who can eat or who can have enjoyment?
> (Ecclesiastes 2:24–25)

Because vocation and recreation are naturally interrelated, we will
treat them together. We can start by asking ourselves these questions:
◇ Where am I on the work and recreation spectrum?
◇ What accounts for any imbalances?

Workaholism and neglect of recreation can be rooted in per-
fectionism, materialism, ambition, insecurity (wounded self-image
compensated for by vocational exploits), expectations and pressures
in the work environment, family culture or ethnic influences, and
escape from unpleasant circumstances in our personal life. Among
the reasons for an underdeveloped work ethic are family culture,
immaturity, negative work experiences, and lack of opportunity, self-
confidence, motivation, and interest.

The most fundamental statement about the relationship of work
and leisure in the Judeo-Christian tradition is contained in the open-
ing chapters of the Book of Genesis. Both Priestly (chapter 1) and
Yahwist (chapter 2) creation narratives speak of the fundamental
goodness and order of both human and divine work.

Work was part of humanity's vocation from the beginning: Adam,
Cain, and Abel engage in their respective chores, with Eve at their side
as a helper who also brings life into the world. Eve has double duty!

With human disobedience, however, birth pangs intensify, women
experience potential domination by men and their own instincts, and

thorns and thistles burst forth to disturb the correspondence between work efforts and results (see Genesis 3:16–19). The human experience of vocation and work as demeaning and onerous, and the adversarial and degenerative aspects of life, are rooted in individual and collective sinfulness rather than in the original divine plan.

Christian teaching throughout the centuries, most recently Pope John Paul II's encyclical *On Human Work,* affirms that work offers us the opportunity to participate in God's creative activity. The Christian's challenge is to avoid becoming discouraged by the drudgery and bitterness of work and vocation, and to cooperate with God in letting it be creative and redemptive. The suffering we experience during work can be allied with Christ's, and can contribute to the completion of the paschal mystery in us (see Colossians 1:24).

Reflection Questions

◇ How have my work experiences, temperament, and family culture affected my work ethic and attitude?
◇ Am I satisfied with the amount of time I devote to work or vocational activities? If not, how would I like to change the quantity, quality, or focus?
◇ Do I pursue continuing education opportunities, read books, or listen to audiotapes that will further my creative experience of and capacity for work?
◇ Do I allocate an appropriate amount of time for recreational activities? If not, why?
◇ When I engage in leisure activities, do I enjoy myself or do I think about work?
◇ Do I select leisure activities that are relaxing rather than chronically competitive and productive?

Action Responses

◇ Cultivate creative attitudes and goals at work to make your situation more fulfilling and less frustrating and stressful.
◇ When you find work becoming drudgery, brainstorm steps to make your job more interesting (for example, set personal goals for growth or productivity, or get away for a while to come back refreshed).

◇ Build into your budget and schedule activities in which you can relax, refrain from pressurized competition, re-energize, and enjoy yourself.

◇ When you leave work physically, leave work psychologically. Sometimes an intermediary activity such as physical exercise can help you work the stressors out before you get home.

34

◆◆◆

Diet

Better is a dinner of vegetables where love is
than a fatted ox and hatred with it.

(Proverbs 15:17)

Better is a dry morsel with quiet
than a house full of feasting with strife.

(Proverbs 17:1)

Food and drink are meant as sustenance and gift rather than as an
escape, outlet, or self-inflicted punishment. When we are stressed or
preoccupied with pressing concerns, our natural compulsion is to
wolf down food and drink before our senses can enjoy them and
monitor their intake. Our mental and spiritual anguish flows into the
physical realm. This perpetuates the anxiety cycle through the physiological discomfort and damage it causes, and the resultant frustration
we experience over our decline in fitness and dietary self-discipline.

A few moments of silence, meditation, or deep breathing before
a meal can help us to eat slowly and with a heightened awareness of
the sensory pleasures of eating. If possible, we might garnish our food
with conversation. Reading at mealtime is detrimental if it interferes
with conversation or sensory enjoyment.

When eating, why not take our time and enjoy? Genesis 1:29 and
2:16 tell us of God's good pleasure in creating physical nourishment
for our sustenance and enjoyment. Genesis 2:9 proclaims the capacity
of food to delight us both sensually and aesthetically. Food and drink
should give us energy rather than heartburn. They should nourish
rather than bloat us.

Reflection Questions

◇ Do I cultivate awareness and make a natural effort to eat slowly and enjoy food and drink?

◇ Do I view shared meals as a sacred event of fellowship and celebration? Do I prioritize such meals in my schedule, especially with family members?

◇ Do I tend toward foods that are healthy or unhealthy nutritionally? Can I take some steps to improve my diet? How do I feel after meal or snack time—bloated, refreshed, or somewhere in between? Can I identify unhealthy patterns that can be replaced with healthier practices?

Action Responses

◇ Adjust your food shopping and consumption patterns to make your diet more healthy and enjoyable. Affirm or reward yourself as you work toward consumption awareness, sensory appreciation, dietary balance, and moderation.

◇ Develop a taste for fruits, grains, and vegetables. Cook and present them in an appetizing manner. Have them available at snack time. If you eat nonnutritious food, combine it with healthy food so that you fill up on the more nutritious items.

35

◆ ◆ ◆

Exercise

> Train yourself in godliness, for, while physical training is of some value, godliness is valuable in every way, holding promise for both the present life and the life to come. (1 Timothy 4:7–8)

Instead of taking your frustrations out on yourself or others, sweat them out.

One of the first things I ask folks who are stressed is, "Are you getting sufficient exercise?" Long working hours and busy schedules are not a legitimate excuse for chronic neglect of exercise. You will fulfill your responsibilities and enjoy life more if you are in decent physical condition. Also, exercise relaxes us, gets the tensions out of our system, and clears out the cobwebs.

The type of exercise depends on the person. Consult your doctor or personal trainer. I love walking and swimming, and enjoy low-impact aerobics. I can walk five miles with a friend and never get bored or tired. The conversation distracts me from the energy I am expending. Whereas many people work out in their homes, I find it enjoyable to go to the local gym and be with others.

Exercise is one of the simplest ways of transforming stress into positive energy. It doesn't have to be competitive exercise. I never count laps when I swim because I don't want to put unnecessary pressure on myself. It is enough of an effort to make it to the pool, let alone hold myself to the standards that were acceptable in my youth.

The body is the temple of the Holy Spirit, and is intimately connected with the mind and spirit. Let's take care of it and encourage our loved ones to do the same.

Reflection Questions

◇ If I don't get sufficient exercise, what are the reasons? What practical steps can I take to get on the right path?

◇ Is there someone I could work out with?

◇ If I am in an exercise routine, do I take it too seriously and thereby make it stressful?

Action Responses

◇ Find a type of exercise that you enjoy, and do it consistently and in a way that is not burdensome.

◇ If it is feasible, take walks with others—your spouse or romantic interest, children, parents, siblings, friends. If you have access, take walks in the woods or by a lake, stream, or ocean.

36

◆ ◆ ◆

Family Values

Each of you, however, should love his wife as himself, and a wife should respect her husband.

Children, obey your parents in the Lord, for this is right. "Honor your father and mother"—this is the first commandment with a promise: "so that it may be well with you and you may live long on the earth."

And, fathers, do not provoke your children to anger, but bring them up in the discipline and instruction of the Lord. (Ephesians 5:33—6:4)

The breakdown of the modern family structure is a well-documented reality that contributes greatly to our inability to cope with stress. We all need support and occasional pep talks, and usually no one is more qualified to provide this than our family members.

The individuals who are most aware of the importance of family are typically those who have been deprived of it. For those of us who are blessed with family members, it is time to wake up, appreciate the gift of family, and renew our participation in the depths and challenges of these relationships.

Jesus did not have an easy family life. Matthew and Luke tell us that it began with perceived adultery, persecutions, and hazardous travel. Misunderstandings occurred among the Holy Family (see, for example, Luke 2:41–51 and John 2:1–11).

Furthermore, we can assume that Joseph died before Jesus' public ministry, leaving Mary a widow. Joseph had a tough life, a fact that usually goes unnoticed. His wife and son never sinned, and before his marriage he was given seemingly impeccable data that his betrothed had been unfaithful. According to Catholic Tradition, his marriage to Mary was never physically consummated.

Saint Joseph is a model for all Christians, particularly men, and a witness to the importance of justice and mercy. The intimacy and confidentiality of family life must be preserved in a spirit of love and mercy.

The Gospels tell us that at various points Jesus' relatives and neighbors thought that he was out of his mind or possessed by an evil spirit. Mary's heart was pierced with a sword as she experienced the Passion of Jesus firsthand. She felt the pain of confusion over God's plan, just as we do. The Holy Family had tremendous stressors. Why should *we* be exempt? They can be a source of inspiration and intercession for us as we struggle for love and peace in these most intimate of relationships.

Reflection Questions

◇ Where does my family rank on my priority list? Am I satisfied with this? Do I devote adequate time, energy, and resources to family life and relationships?

◇ If I could improve my family relationships in some way, with whom would I start and how would I go about it? What specific attitudes and actions would I embrace? What obstacles might I encounter in trying to improve family relationships? How might I anticipate and prepare for them?

◇ Could I benefit from pastoral care, spiritual direction, or psychological therapy?

Action Responses

◇ Do something loving each day for a loved one. Overlook the petty comment made out of frustration, or the immature action committed by a stressed loved one.

◇ Consistently build ample quality time into your schedule for family activities. What is more important than family? Visit or telephone family members who are lonely.

37

◆◆◆

Permission
and
Prohibition

> The LORD God took the man and put him in the garden of Eden
> to till it and keep it. And the LORD God commanded the man,
> "You may freely eat of every tree of the garden; but of the tree of
> the knowledge of good and evil you shall not eat, for in the day
> that you eat of it you shall die." (Genesis 2:15–17)

The moral and natural boundaries alluded to in the above passage
from Genesis are relevant to our discussion. Distortions of these values
can compromise our ability to discern between controllable and
uncontrollable stressors.

The essence of the divine prohibition is that we are free and responsible, but not autonomous, creatures. The exact meaning of the
phrase "knowledge of good and evil" is debated by scholars, but the
general consensus seems to be that it is a *merism*, an inclusive way of
expressing the totality of something by way of two extreme parts, such
as "from A to Z" or "from young to old." From this perspective, "knowledge of good and evil" means more than simply omniscience or moral
autonomy; it refers to the divine ability to comprehend and experience everything truthfully and wholesomely, and to reconcile oppo-
sites; in other words, to be God, the master of all reality.

The ability to comprehend and cope successfully with the para-
doxes and contradictions of semiautonomous human existence is a
divine prerogative that cannot be appropriated by human grasping
(see Philippians 2:6). All we do when we step outside the circle of
obedience is to create stressors for all concerned. Because of original
and personal sin, we now must contend with stressors created by
grasping not of our own making, resulting in innocent suffering.

In the Genesis narrative, God's prohibition of divine experiential knowledge and the moral precepts and inherent punishments derived from it are real and unexplained, but in our best interests.

Not being satisfied with what is permissible, we begin to contemplate and desire what lies outside our boundaries. In our preoccupation with autonomous success, we overlook the other half of God's precept, the invitation to exercise dominion and creativity and to partake of the earth's goodness. How much happier we would be if we strived to be content with what we have, and to live within our means and limitations.

We all need to exercise our God-given permission to have dominion over the earth and enjoy the good things of life. The many permissible trees (in the symbolic language of Genesis), which have the qualities to satisfy us (Genesis 2:9), can help us cope with stressors and find positive alternatives to the temptations and obstacles we experience.

Failure to take advantage of these permissible gifts can lead to angelism (trying to be angels rather than bodily creatures), puritanism, moral rigidity, or scrupulosity, and their accompanying conscious and subconscious stressors.

In healthy tension with permissibility is the human need for prohibitions. Some things are not constructive or appropriate; we need guidelines and limitations. Failure to respect this leads to liberality and unconstrained behavior and, inevitably, stress.

Reflection Questions

◇ Am I scrupulous and spartan in certain areas? Do I sometimes resist life's invitation to enjoy myself? Are there areas and circumstances in which I fail to partake of the gifts God gives me in the form of myself, nature, the material world, or other persons? Do I exacerbate some limitations, restrictions, and trials by failing to take advantage of coping mechanisms that God and life provide?

◇ What scruples, conditioning, attitudes, past experiences, or inner voices compel me to resist the freedom, gifts, and joy God gratuitously offers me? What do I think accounts for my tendencies?

◇ Conversely, am I morally lax in certain areas at the expense of myself or others? Are there areas in which I habitually or compulsively overstep my bounds and limitations in an obsessive pursuit of perfection, satisfaction, or personal goals? How might I exercise greater prudence and responsibility? What resources of the church or society will help me balance permission and prohibition?

Action Responses

◇ As the need appears, take small steps to more harmoniously accept natural and moral boundaries and your own limitations.
◇ Find small ways you can loosen up a little and enjoy life's permissible pleasures, to your own and others' benefit.

Closing Synthesis

It was fitting to end with a meditation on the Beginning and the time-less spiritual and moral challenge the Genesis story narrates. Unhealthy stress ultimately can be tied to transgression of boundaries and misuse of God's creation. Making good choices amid temptations is difficult. Suffering because of our own and others' bad choices is an inherent stressor in life.

We can allow God to bring good out of these negative experiences, or we can become hardened. As conveyed in Matthew 25:31–46 (the parable of the sheep and goats), if we try to love God, others, and ourselves, we will transform stress and suffering into love. "We know that all things work together for good for those who love God, who are called according to his purpose" (Romans 8:28). God is ultimately the best stress transformation helper.

Building each other up (through affirmations) and dialoguing with God and neighbor are among the most practical of stress trans-formers, and are within reach of all of us.

I introduced *lectio divina* because of the importance of wrestling with God's word and having it penetrate our whole being. Like Job, we need deep personal contact with God that goes beyond words: "I had heard of you by the hearing of the ear, / but now my eye sees you" (Job 42:5). Affirmations remind us of what we often forget: the sub-conscious mind must be cultivated and placed in submission to God's will, just like the rest of us.

In its submission to God's will, Christianity differs from human potential philosophy and materialistic approaches to stress manage-ment. A Christian approach to stress is inherently nuanced, moderat-ed, and predicated on moral and spiritual considerations. It must pay attention to the human sciences, but not be dominated by them.

Some of our decisions will bring us more, rather than less, stress because of the higher principle involved. If Jesus' only goal was to be healthy, he would have gone about life differently. Both he and we have a mission that includes taking responsibility for our health and stress levels, but not to make idols out of them. God's will be done, even to the point of laying down our life for one another and for God's saving plan.

Jesus told his followers, "See, I am sending you out like sheep into the midst of wolves; so be wise as serpents and innocent as doves" (Matthew 10:16). May we exercise love, courage, wisdom, and discretion in fulfilling the two commandments we ultimately have to concern ourselves with: loving God with our whole selves, and its derivative, loving our neighbor as ourselves.

If we keep these two precepts in mind as we apply the insights we have gained in reading, praying, and living this book, we will keep ourselves occupied with serving God and one another. Our stressors will be transformed inherently, in God's way and time, both directly and through the back door.

> Those who find their life will lose it, and those who lose their life for my sake will find it. (Matthew 10:39)

> I have said this to you, so that in me you may have peace. In the world you face persecution. But take courage; I have conquered the world! (John 16:33)

Bibliography

Benson, Herbert. *The Relaxation Response.* New York: Avon Books, 1975.

Benson, Herbert, and William Proctor. *Beyond the Relaxation Response.* New York: Times Books, 1984.

Green, Thomas H. *Drinking from a Dry Well.* Notre Dame, IN: Ave Maria Press, 1991.

———. *When the Well Runs Dry.* Notre Dame, IN: Ave Maria Press, 1979.

Guigo II. *The Ladder of Monks and Twelve Meditations.* Translated by Edmund Colledge, OSA, and James Walsh, SJ. Kalamazoo, MI: Cistercian Publications, 1981.

Hall, Thelma. *Too Deep for Words: Rediscovering Lectio Divina.* Mahwah, NJ: Paulist Press, 1988.

Helmstetter, Shad. *The Self-Talk Solution.* New York: Pocket Books, 1987.

————. *What to Say When You Talk to Yourself.* New York: Pocket Books, 1986.

Heschel, Abraham Joshua. *The Sabbath.* New York: Farrar, Straus, and Giroux, 1951.

Keating, Thomas. *Invitation to Love.* Rockport, MA: Element Books, 1992.

————. *The Mystery of Christ.* Rockport, MA: Element Books, 1991.

————. *Open Heart, Open Mind.* Rockport, MA: Element Books, 1986.

Leclercq, Dom Jean. *The Love of Learning and the Desire for God.* New York: Mentor Omega Books, 1962.

Michael, Chester P., and Marie C. Norrisey. *Prayer and Temperament.* Charlottesville, VA: The Open Door, 1984.

Mork, Wulstan. *The Benedictine Way.* Petersham, MA: Saint Bede's Publications, 1987.

Muto, Susan. *A Practical Guide to Spiritual Reading.* Petersham, MA: Saint Bede's Publications, 1994.

Muto, Susan, and Adrian vanKaam. *Harnessing Stress.* Williston Park, NY: Resurrection Press, 1993.

————. *Healthy and Holy Under Stress.* Williston Park, NY: Resurrection Press, 1993.

————. *Stress and the Search for Happiness.* Williston Park, NY: Resurrection Press, 1993.

O'Rourke, Robert D. *Prescriptions for Stress.* Allen, TX: Argus Communications, 1982.

Schultz, Karl A. *The Art and Vocation of Caring for People in Pain.* Mahwah, NJ: Paulist Press, 1993.

————. *Job Therapy.* Pittsburgh: Genesis Personal Development Center, 1996.

————. *Journaling with Moses and Job.* Boston: Saint Paul Books and Media, 1996.

————. *Nourished by the Word.* Notre Dame, IN: Ave Maria Press, 1994.

————. *Personal Energy Management.* Chicago: Loyola University Press, 1994.

————. *Personal Energy Manager Rainbow Planner.* Pittsburgh: Genesis Personal Development Center, 1996.

————. *Where Is God When You Need Him? Sharing Stories of Suffering with Job and Jesus.* New York: Alba House, 1992.

Shannon, William H. *Seeking the Face of God.* New York: Crossroad, 1988.